# FEEDING TIME at the ZOO

# SHERRY SHAHAN

*Especially for Keeper Lisa Conklin*
*and my friends at Charles Paddock Zoo*

A Random House PICTUREBACK® Book

Random House 🏛 New York

Copyright © 2000 by Sherry Shahan. All rights reserved under International and Pan-American Copyright Conventions. Published in the United States by Random House, Inc., New York, and simultaneously in Canada by Random House of Canada Limited, Toronto.
www.randomhouse.com/kids
*Library of Congress Cataloging-in-Publication Data*
Shahan, Sherry.  Feeding time at the zoo / by Sherry Shahan.  p.  cm. — (A Random House pictureback)
SUMMARY: Simple text and photographs depict a variety of zoo animals at feeding time, as well as the food-related activities of zoo staff.
ISBN 0-375-80067-0 (pbk.)
1. Zoo animals—Food—Juvenile literature.  2. Zoo animals—Feeding and feeds—Juvenile literature.  [1. Zoo animals—Food.
2. Zoo animals—Feeding and Feeds.]  I. Title.  II. Series.  QL77.5.S46  2000  636.088'9—dc21  98-18468
Printed in the United States of America    June 2000    10  9  8  7  6  5  4  3  2  1
PICTUREBACK, RANDOM HOUSE and colophon, and PLEASE READ TO ME and colophon are registered trademarks of Random House, Inc.

It's feeding time at the zoo!

The zookeeper has peeled and sliced and diced all morning.

Now she loads the food cart and brings breakfast to the animals.

Elephants get timothy hay. Timothy hay is a type of tall grass that is cut, dried, and bundled into bales. This elephant likes his hay a little moist. He drops it in the water for a quick soak—just like cereal in milk!

Elephants can eat 150 pounds of food a day.
They eat hay, grain, bran, and even watermelons!

Zebras and giraffes also eat hay.

For snacks, they nibble on the leaves of plants.

This giraffe has room to roam in her grassland home. After breakfast, she gets a drink of water from the pond.

Zookeepers work hard to keep the animals happy and healthy. This spider monkey gets a children's chewable vitamin—just like the ones you might take.

In the wild, animals have to search for their food. So to keep the spider monkeys from getting bored, the zookeeper hides apples, oranges, and sunflower snacks for them to find.

Polar bears get to look for their food, too.

The zookeeper throws pieces of raw vegetables into the water for snacks. This polar bear dives in and comes up with a sweet potato treat.

It's time for breakfast!
The polar bear gets fresh
fish, fruit, and rice.
    After breakfast, it's time
to settle down for a nap.

The giant panda likes bamboo. She strips the woody stalks of their tender leaves before eating them. The bamboo is grown right at the zoo, so it is always fresh!

Many animals need to eat their vegetables—just like people!

The potbellied pig eats a bowl of peppers, squash, tomatoes, carrots, and lettuce. When he eats corn on the cob, he eats the whole thing— corncob and all!

The tortoise gets a vegetable salad with special "leaf-eater" biscuits chopped in. Can you guess how these biscuits got their name? They have all the nutrients that plant-eating animals need to stay healthy. Each biscuit is only as big around as a pencil!

Tortoise's Salad

2 lbs. carrots, coarsely ground
8 oz. apples
1 lb. each cucumber and squash
1⅓ lbs. combined spinach and kale
1⅓ lbs. dry rabbit chow with water added

Porcupines get a
healthy mix of spinach,
sweet potatoes, fruit,
raisins, and leaf-eater food.
This porcupine nibbles
on a peeled banana.

*I'm hungry!* roars the tiger.

The tiger is a meat-eater. The zookeeper feeds her a bucket of giant meatballs with vitamins and minerals mixed in.

After breakfast, the tiger stretches and licks herself clean. Then she struts into her yard and relaxes under a shady tree.

Do animals use knives and forks? No! But sometimes they do eat off utensils.

*Chomp!* The alligator snatches a meatball off a broom. If a broom "spoon" wasn't used, the meat would fall apart in the water.

The sea lion is a fish-eater.
*Arf! Arf!* He sits up and barks
for his breakfast.

Breakfast for the birds is as colorful as the birds themselves.

A cockatoo sizes up a whole carrot.

A macaw peels a juicy orange.

Shredding and peeling food keeps the birds busy. Later, they will eat their main meal—a mixture of bird feed and seeds.

Flamingoes eat with
their heads upside down.
They use their beaks to
scoop up small shellfish,
worms, and seeds from
the water.

Their bright pink color
comes from the shellfish
they eat.

Visitors can feed the animals snacks in the petting zoo.

Kids hold out ice cream cones filled with crunchy food pellets. Come and get it!

Later, the petting zoo closes and the animals eat a hearty hay meal.

All this food
is enough to make
anyone hungry!
    What do you think
the kids at the zoo
will have for a snack?
    Hay? Bamboo?
Leaf-eater biscuits?
    No! Tutti-frutti
ice cream pops!